Glimpse of Moon; Means You

Mrigendra Bharti

Published by Sellbrochure Entertainment Vymish, 2024.

GLIMPSE OF MOON; MEANS YOU

First edition. June 2, 2024.

ISBN: 979-8227765659

Written by Mrigendra Bharti.

Preface:

In the boundless expanse of human emotion and artistic expression, we find ourselves drawn to the ineffable allure of admiration. Within these pages, I humbly embark upon a poetic journey, seeking to articulate the depth of reverence inspired by a singular presence. This collection of verses serves as a homage to the enigmatic essence of one whose influence transcends the ordinary, shaping the very fabric of our perceptions. As we delve into the intricacies of admiration, may these words serve as a tribute to the enduring power of beauty and grace.

Foreword:

In the vast expanse of poetic endeavor, we embark upon a journey of homage, a voyage through the corridors of admiration. Here, within the pages of verse, we endeavor to capture the essence of one whose presence ignites the embers of our souls. With each syllable, we strive to encapsulate the profundity of feeling, the depth of reverence, and the sheer awe inspired by her being. Let these words serve as a testament to the indelible mark she has left upon our hearts, a beacon of light in the vast expanse of existence.

Prologue:

Amidst the tapestry of human emotions, in the symphony of life's unfolding drama, we pause to embark upon a literary odyssey. In the genesis of this poetic narrative, we lay the foundation of admiration, casting our gaze upon a figure whose presence commands reverence. Here, in the sanctum of verse, we endeavor to illuminate the essence of one who captivates hearts with her mere existence. Let these lines serve as an overture to the eloquent prose that follows, a prelude to the enigmatic portrait we shall paint in words, paying homage to the ineffable beauty that graces our world.

Acknowledgement:

In the pursuit of poetic homage, we stand indebted to the muses who inspire our pen to dance upon the canvas of words. To those whose ethereal presence infuses our verses with meaning and beauty, we offer our heartfelt gratitude. With reverence, we acknowledge the guiding light of inspiration that illuminates our path, shaping our words into tributes of admiration. May our humble offerings serve as a testament to the profound impact of your being on our creative journey.

Dedication:

To the embodiment of elegance and grace, whose presence inspires the very essence of this literary endeavor, I dedicate these words. In the vast expanse of admiration and reverence, your influence transcends mere description, guiding the hand that pens these verses. In the pages that follow, may the spirit of your beauty and charm resonate, as a timeless testament to the profound impact you have on those fortunate enough to be touched by your presence.

Introduction:

In the realm of admiration and reverence, where the pen dances upon the parchment to honor the sublime, we find ourselves at the threshold of a literary journey. Within these pages, we embark upon a quest to encapsulate the essence of a soul whose presence resonates with the profound. In this introductory passage, we set the stage for a poetic exploration, weaving words into tapestries of admiration, as we pay homage to the enigmatic allure of our subject. Join us as we delve into the intricacies of admiration and adoration, seeking to capture the ineffable beauty that graces our hearts and minds.

Her Words

In an enigmatic smile,
Her words, a unique style,
Every moment by her side,
In the heartbeat, she resides.
Getting lost in her gaze,
Her world, a fragrant maze,
Every moment, her memory,
A desire deep within me.
In her smile's grace,
A story my heart does embrace,
How can I express,
The elegance of her finesse.
In every word she speaks,
Hidden love it seeks,
A voice from the heart,
The reality of praising her art.

In Her Radiance

In her radiance, a tale untold,
A beauty beyond, a sight to behold.
Every glance, a whispered dream,
In her aura, a celestial gleam.
With each smile, the world takes flight,
Her words, a symphony of light.
In every moment, her essence divine,
In her presence, love's sweet wine.
Lost in her eyes, a universe explored,
Her essence, a fragrance adored.
In her presence, a silent plea,
To capture her grace eternally.

Enigmatic Beauty

In the silence of a whispering breeze,
Resides a beauty that words can't seize.
In her eyes, the stars find their home,
Guiding lost souls, no longer to roam.
Her smile, a melody, pure and true,
Bringing light to skies of deepest blue.
Each step she takes, a dance divine,
Enchanting hearts, like aged wine.
In her presence, time takes flight,
Moments shared, a treasure bright.
Her laughter, a symphony of delight,
Filling the air with pure delight.
A portrait of grace, painted in hues,
In every glance, a tale ensues.
Though mere words may fall short,
Her essence, a masterpiece of sorts.
So here I pen this humble rhyme,
In homage to her, beyond space and time.
For in her radiance, I find my muse,
A timeless beauty, I cannot refuse.

An Ode to Grace

In the whispers of the night's soft embrace,
Resides a beauty, adorned with grace.
Her presence, a gentle melody,
In every glance, a symphony.
In her eyes, the stars find their reflection,
A celestial dance, a divine connection.
With each step, she paints the sky,
In hues of wonder, catching every eye.
Her smile, a beacon in the dark,
Igniting hope with its spark.
Her laughter, like a soothing song,
In its melody, hearts belong.
With words, I seek to express,
The depth of admiration, the tenderness.
Yet, in her presence, I find,
Language fails, and thoughts unwind.
So here I offer this humble verse,
In homage to her, an eternal curse.
For in her, beauty finds its home,
A muse divine, never to roam.

In the Presence of Grace

In the tapestry of life, a portrait is drawn,
Of a soul adorned with grace, like the dawn.
With each sunrise, her beauty does bloom,
Casting shadows of awe in every room.
Her laughter, a melody that fills the air,
A symphony of joy beyond compare.
In her presence, time seems to stand still,
As every moment with her is a thrill.
Her kindness, a beacon in the night,
Guiding lost souls towards the light.
In her eyes, the universe is reflected,
A cosmic dance, infinitely connected.
With each word spoken, her wisdom flows,
Like a river that endlessly grows.
In her embrace, fears are allayed,
And dreams of tomorrow are safely laid.
So here, in this verse, I humbly pay,
Homage to her, in every way.
For she is the embodiment of love's art,
A masterpiece engraved upon my heart.

Enchanted by Her Aura

In the tranquil embrace of night's gentle breeze,
Lies a beauty adorned with effortless ease.
Her presence, a symphony of grace and charm,
In her aura, I find myself disarm.
With each smile, she paints the sky anew,
A canvas of hues, both vibrant and true.
Her laughter, like the sweetest melody,
Echoes through the air, setting spirits free.
In her eyes, the secrets of the universe reside,
A mesmerizing gaze, where dreams coincide.
With every word, she weaves a tale divine,
Captivating hearts, like vintage wine.
In her touch, I find solace and peace,
A sanctuary where worries cease.
In her embrace, I find sanctuary,
Lost in the depths of her boundless beauty.
So here, in this ode, I humbly express,
Adoration for her, in its purest finesse.
For she is the muse that inspires my art,
Enchanted by her aura, I surrender my heart.

Whispers of Elegance

In whispers soft, the night reveals,
A beauty that every heart steals.
With every step, she graces the earth,
A vision of elegance, of immeasurable worth.
Her laughter, a melody in the air,
A symphony of joy, beyond compare.
In her eyes, the stars find their place,
Reflecting the wonder of her grace.
With each word spoken, wisdom flows,
A river of knowledge that endlessly grows.
In her presence, worries fade away,
Lost in the warmth of her gentle sway.
Her kindness, a beacon in the dark,
Guiding souls to find their spark.
In her embrace, fears find release,
As she fills every moment with peace.
So here, in this verse, I attempt to convey,
The depth of my admiration, day by day.
For she is the epitome of elegance and grace,
A vision that time cannot erase.

Whispers of the Heart

In the whispers of the heart, a tale unfolds,
Of a beauty whose essence, forever holds.
With every glance, a story untold,
In her presence, mysteries unfold.
Her smile, a beacon in the night,
Guiding lost souls towards the light.
In her laughter, echoes of joy resound,
A symphony of happiness, profound.
In her eyes, the depths of oceans lie,
Reflecting the beauty of the sky.
With every word, she paints the air,
A masterpiece of love and care.
Her kindness, a gentle breeze that soothes,
Healing wounds with its tender moves.
In her embrace, fears fade away,
Lost in the warmth of her gentle sway.
So here, in this verse, I quietly pay,
Homage to her, in every way.
For she is the melody of my soul's song,
In her presence, I forever belong.

In the Whispering Wind

In whispers soft, the night unveils,
A beauty that every heart hails.
With each step, she graces the ground,
In elegance, a treasure found.
Her laughter, a melody so sweet,
In its joy, hearts find their beat.
In her eyes, the stars find their gleam,
Reflecting the beauty of a dream.
With each word she speaks, a tale is spun,
In her presence, sorrows undone.
In her touch, warmth and grace,
A sanctuary in life's race.
Her kindness, a light in the dark,
Guiding souls with its gentle spark.
In her embrace, fears take flight,
Lost in the comfort, all feels right.
So here, in this verse, I aim to convey,
The depth of admiration, come what may.
For she is the essence of beauty and art,
Forever engraved in the whispers of the heart.

In the Silhouette of Grace

In the silhouette of grace, she stands,
A vision crafted by tender hands.
With each smile, she paints the day,
In hues of joy, leading the way.
Her laughter, a melody in the air,
Filling hearts with warmth and care.
In her eyes, secrets softly hide,
Reflecting depths, worlds inside.
With each word, she weaves a spell,
In her presence, all is well.
In her touch, comfort is found,
In her embrace, peace surrounds.
Her kindness, a guiding light,
In darkness, shining bright.
In her essence, beauty flows,
A river of love that forever grows.
So here, in this verse, I endeavor to say,
Admiration for her, in every way.
For she is the epitome of grace,
In her presence, the heart finds its place.

Beneath the Moonlit Sky

Beneath the moonlit sky, she glows,
A radiant beauty, the world knows.
With each step, she treads with grace,
In her presence, time and space erase.
Her laughter, a melody divine,
Echoes through the night, like wine.
In her eyes, the stars find a home,
Guiding lost souls, no longer to roam.
With every word, she paints a scene,
In her aura, serenity's glean.
In her touch, comfort abides,
In her embrace, all fear subsides.
Her kindness, a beacon bright,
In darkness, offering light.
In her being, love does bloom,
In her essence, the heart finds room.
So here, in this ode, I humbly express,
The admiration for her, in its finesse.
For she is the muse of my heart's cry,
Beneath the moonlit sky.

Her Laughter

In whispers soft, her presence graces,
A vision of beauty, in all its phases.
With each smile, she lights the way,
In her glow, darkness can't stay.
Her laughter, a melody so pure,
In its echo, souls find a cure.
In her eyes, the universe unfolds,
Secrets whispered, tales untold.
With every word, she casts a spell,
In her aura, all is well.
In her touch, comfort reigns,
In her embrace, love sustains.
Her kindness, a guiding star,
In her warmth, all fears depart.
In her being, love finds a home,
In her essence, hearts roam.
So here, in this verse, I quietly impart,
Adoration for her, straight from the heart.
For she is the muse of my creation,
In her, I find endless fascination.

Song of Reverence

In the symphony of life's grand ballet,
She pirouettes, in elegant display.
With every twirl, a tale she weaves,
In her grace, the heart believes.
Her laughter, a sonnet in the breeze,
Bringing solace, putting minds at ease.
In her gaze, the moon finds its gleam,
Reflecting the depth of a timeless dream.
With every word, she paints a rhyme,
In her presence, transcending time.
In her embrace, worries take flight,
Lost in the warmth of her guiding light.
Her kindness, a beacon in the night,
Illuminating paths, shining bright.
In her being, love finds its wings,
In her essence, the soul sings.
So here, in this ode, I softly sing,
A melody of admiration, to her I bring.
For she is the muse of my poetic art,
In her, I find solace, and a fresh start.

In the Aura of Wonder

In the aura of wonder, she resides,
A symphony of beauty, that abides.
With each step, she graces the earth,
In her presence, all doubts find rebirth.
Her laughter, a cascade of joyous sound,
Echoes through the air, profound.
In her eyes, the secrets of galaxies twirl,
Enchanting hearts, like a precious pearl.
With every word, she spins a tale,
In her essence, dreams set sail.
In her touch, serenity is found,
In her embrace, worries are unbound.
Her kindness, a beacon in the night,
Guiding lost souls towards the light.
In her being, love takes flight,
In her essence, everything feels right.
So here, in this verse, I humbly convey,
Adoration for her, in every way.
For she is the embodiment of grace,
In her presence, the world finds its place.

In the Glow of Her Aura

In the glow of her aura, a marvel unfolds,
A vision of beauty, endlessly told.
With each step, she paints the ground,
In her presence, harmony is found.
Her laughter, a melody, sweet and pure,
Bringing solace, an everlasting cure.
In her eyes, the stars find their light,
Guiding lost souls through the night.
With every word, she weaves a tale,
In her essence, dreams set sail.
In her touch, a gentle breeze,
In her embrace, all worries cease.
Her kindness, a beacon, shining bright,
In her warmth, darkness takes flight.
In her being, love finds its home,
In her essence, we cease to roam.
So here, in this ode, I humbly impart,
Admiration for her, straight from the heart.
For she is the epitome of grace and allure,
In her presence, the world feels pure.

In Her Radiance

In her radiance, a tapestry of awe,
A beauty beyond measure, with no flaw.
With each smile, she lights up the sky,
In her presence, all troubles say goodbye.
Her laughter, a melody of delight,
Filling hearts with warmth, day and night.
In her eyes, the universe unfurls,
Revealing secrets, in precious pearls.
With every word, she casts a spell,
In her essence, all is well.
In her touch, comfort finds its place,
In her embrace, fears do erase.
Her kindness, a beacon in the dark,
Guiding souls to find their spark.
In her being, love blooms like a flower,
In her essence, we find our power.
So here, in this verse, I humbly convey,
Adoration for her, in every way.
For she is the epitome of grace and light,
In her presence, everything feels right.

In Her Majesty's Aura

In her majesty's aura, a realm divine,
Resides a beauty, like the stars that shine.
With each step, she paints the earth anew,
In her presence, dreams find a breakthrough.
Her laughter, a symphony of joy and mirth,
Bringing solace to souls, giving them rebirth.
In her eyes, the universe finds its reflection,
A kaleidoscope of wonder, beyond comprehension.
With every word, she weaves tales untold,
In her essence, mysteries unfold.
In her touch, serenity takes flight,
In her embrace, all fears take flight.
Her kindness, a beacon in the night's expanse,
Guiding hearts with its gentle dance.
In her being, love finds its eternal flame,
In her essence, we find solace, untamed.
So here, in this verse, I quietly convey,
Admiration for her, in every possible way.
For she is the epitome of grace and allure,
In her presence, all is pure and sure.

Reflections of Admiration

In the reflection of her radiant grace,
A marvel of beauty, a timeless embrace.
With each breath, she paints the sky,
In her presence, all worries pass by.
Her laughter, a melody so sweet,
In its cadence, hearts find their beat.
In her eyes, the universe takes flight,
Revealing wonders in the darkest night.
With every word, she spins a tale,
In her essence, dreams never pale.
In her touch, serenity finds its place,
In her embrace, fears do efface.
Her kindness, a beacon in the night,
Guiding souls towards the light.
In her being, love finds its home,
In her essence, we cease to roam.
So here, in this verse, I quietly convey,
Admiration for her, in every way.
For she is the muse of my poetic art,
In her presence, I find solace, a fresh start.

In the Whispering Winds

In the whispering winds, her essence sways,
A symphony of beauty in the sun's gentle rays.
With each step, she graces the earth,
In her aura, a timeless worth.
Her laughter, a melody that dances free,
In its embrace, hearts find glee.
In her eyes, the galaxies align,
Reflecting the depths of a love so divine.
With every word, she paints a dream,
In her presence, nothing's as it seems.
In her touch, comfort softly flows,
In her embrace, peace silently glows.
Her kindness, a beacon in the night,
Guiding lost souls towards the light.
In her being, love finds its prime,
In her essence, we find our rhyme.
So here, in this verse, I humbly impart,
Admiration for her, straight from the heart.
For she is the muse of my soul's sweet song,
In her presence, I feel I belong.

Silent Reverie

In the silent reverie of twilight's glow,
Lies a beauty that only few may know.
With each whispered breeze, she softly sighs,
In her presence, the heart surely flies.
Her laughter, a gentle stream's soft flow,
In its melody, all troubles go.
In her eyes, the stars find their gleam,
Guiding wanderers through life's dream.
With each uttered word, she casts a spell,
In her essence, all is well.
In her touch, serenity finds its way,
In her embrace, worries allay.
Her kindness, a beacon in the night,
Guiding lost souls toward the light.
In her being, love finds its rest,
In her essence, we are blessed.
So here, in this verse, I softly impart,
Admiration for her, from my heart.
For she is the muse of my soul's sweet song,
In her presence, I feel I belong.

Whispers of Enchantment

In whispers soft, her essence weaves,
A tapestry of beauty that never leaves.
With each step, she graces the earth,
In her aura, a timeless rebirth.
Her laughter, a melody so divine,
In its resonance, all troubles resign.
In her eyes, the cosmos finds its reflection,
Revealing secrets beyond mere perception.
With every word, she spins a tale,
In her presence, all worries pale.
In her touch, tranquility gently flows,
In her embrace, serenity grows.
Her kindness, a beacon in the night,
Guiding souls towards the light.
In her being, love finds its home,
In her essence, we cease to roam.
So here, in this verse, I softly convey,
Admiration for her, in every way.
For she is the epitome of grace and charm,
In her presence, the world finds calm.

Echoes of Grace

In the gentle whispers of the breeze,
Resides a beauty that forever frees.
With each graceful step, she bestows,
In her presence, the world aglow.
Her laughter, a symphony of delight,
In its echoes, hearts take flight.
In her eyes, galaxies converge,
A celestial dance, an eternal urge.
With every word, she paints a scene,
In her aura, dreams convene.
In her touch, tranquility's embrace,
In her embrace, fears find solace.
Her kindness, a guiding light,
In the darkest hour, shining bright.
In her being, love takes its form,
In her essence, we weather the storm.
So here, in this verse, I softly impart,
Admiration for her, from my heart.
For she is the muse of my soul's refrain,
In her presence, all is gentle, all is sane.

Serene Symphony

In the serene symphony of dawn's embrace,
Resides a beauty, adorned with grace.
With each whispered breeze, she softly glows,
In her aura, tranquility flows.
Her laughter, a melody of pure delight,
In its resonance, hearts take flight.
In her eyes, the heavens align,
Revealing secrets, both yours and mine.
With every word, she weaves a tale,
In her presence, worries pale.
In her touch, serenity finds its way,
In her embrace, troubles stray.
Her kindness, a beacon in the night,
Guiding lost souls toward the light.
In her being, love finds its home,
In her essence, we cease to roam.
So here, in this verse, I softly express,
Admiration for her, in its finesse.
For she is the muse of my heart's melody,
In her presence, life is sheer ecstasy.

Embrace of Elegance

In the embrace of elegance, she reigns,
A vision of beauty that forever sustains.
With each delicate step, she graces the earth,
In her presence, all finds its worth.
Her laughter, a symphony of joy untold,
In its melody, hearts unfold.
In her eyes, the universe finds its glow,
Reflecting wonders, both high and low.
With every word, she spins a tale divine,
In her aura, dreams intertwine.
In her touch, serenity takes flight,
In her embrace, fears take flight.
Her kindness, a guiding light in the dark,
Leading souls on a journey, like a lark.
In her being, love finds its sanctuary,
In her essence, we find our serenity.
So here, in this verse, I humbly convey,
Admiration for her, day by day.
For she is the epitome of grace,
In her presence, all falls into place.

Whispers of Wonder

In whispers soft, the world does tell,
Of a beauty whose presence casts a spell.
With each gentle step, she graces the ground,
In her aura, enchantment is found.
Her laughter, a melody that fills the air,
In its sweetness, worries disappear.
In her eyes, the stars find their gleam,
Reflecting the beauty of a dream.
With every word, she paints a scene,
In her presence, life feels serene.
In her touch, tranquility does reside,
In her embrace, fears subside.
Her kindness, a beacon in the night,
Guiding lost souls towards the light.
In her being, love finds its abode,
In her essence, we find our road.
So here, in this verse, I softly impart,
Admiration for her, from my heart.
For she is the muse of my reverie,
In her presence, life finds its beauty.

In the Harmony of Her Presence

In the harmony of her presence, a symphony unfolds,
A melody of beauty, a story yet untold.
With each graceful movement, she paints the air,
In her aura, tranquility finds its lair.
Her laughter, a chorus of joyous delight,
In its resonance, hearts take flight.
In her eyes, the universe finds its reflection,
Revealing secrets, a divine connection.
With every word, she weaves a tapestry of dreams,
In her essence, life's complexities gleam.
In her touch, serenity softly flows,
In her embrace, the soul knows.
Her kindness, a guiding light in the night,
Leading hearts toward hope's bright light.
In her being, love finds its home,
In her essence, we cease to roam.
So here, in this verse, I humbly convey,
Admiration for her, in every way.
For she is the muse of my heart's melody,
In her presence, life feels like a sweet reverie.

In Her Radiant Glow

In her radiant glow, the world finds its hue,
A beauty so rare, so endlessly true.
With each step, she paints the earth with grace,
In her presence, time and space embrace.
Her laughter, a melody that dances in the air,
In its sweet notes, all worries disappear.
In her eyes, the stars find their reflection,
Guiding lost souls toward affection.
With every word, she spins tales untold,
In her aura, dreams find foothold.
In her touch, tranquility gently sways,
In her embrace, hearts find solace in the maze.
Her kindness, a beacon in the darkest night,
Leading souls toward the guiding light.
In her being, love finds its dwelling place,
In her essence, the world finds solace and grace.
So here, in this verse, I softly convey,
Admiration for her, in every way.
For she is the muse of my heart's sweet song,
In her presence, all troubles are gone.

Her Majesty's Embrace

In the embrace of her majesty, we find,
A treasure trove of beauty, one of a kind.
With each gentle sway, she paints the sky,
In her presence, all worries bid goodbye.
Her laughter, a melody so sweet and rare,
In its embrace, hearts find repair.
In her eyes, the universe takes its cue,
Revealing wonders, both old and new.
With every word, she crafts tales divine,
In her aura, dreams intertwine.
In her touch, serenity takes flight,
In her embrace, all fears take flight.
Her kindness, a beacon in the night's expanse,
Guiding hearts with its gentle dance.
In her being, love finds its purest form,
In her essence, all troubles are outworn.
So here, in this verse, I softly impart,
Admiration for her, from the depths of my heart.
For she is the muse of my soul's sweet song,
In her presence, we all belong.

In Her Elegance Enshrined

In her elegance enshrined, a marvel unfolds,
A beauty beyond measure, a tale untold.
With each graceful step, she lights the way,
In her presence, darkness fades away.
Her laughter, a melody that fills the air,
In its enchanting rhythm, all worries disappear.
In her eyes, the cosmos finds its reflection,
Revealing the secrets of a divine connection.
With every word, she spins stories of grace,
In her aura, tranquility finds its place.
In her touch, serenity gently flows,
In her embrace, love endlessly grows.
Her kindness, a guiding light in the night,
Leading souls toward hope's eternal light.
In her being, love finds its eternal home,
In her essence, hearts cease to roam.
So here, in this verse, I softly convey,
Admiration for her, in every possible way.
For she is the epitome of elegance and charm,
In her presence, the world finds solace and calm.

In the Tapestry of Grace

In the tapestry of grace, she reigns supreme,
A vision of beauty like a waking dream.
With each gentle movement, she weaves a spell,
In her presence, all is well.
Her laughter, a melody that fills the air,
In its gentle cadence, all troubles disappear.
In her eyes, the stars find their reflection,
Guiding lost souls to their destined direction.
With every word, she paints a picture divine,
In her aura, serenity intertwines.
In her touch, comfort softly flows,
In her embrace, all worries lose their throes.
Her kindness, a beacon in the darkest night,
Guiding weary hearts toward the light.
In her being, love finds its truest form,
In her essence, all find shelter from the storm.
So here, in this verse, I softly impart,
Admiration for her, from the depths of my heart.
For she is the muse of my soul's sweet song,
In her presence, we all belong.

In Her Radiant Aura

In her radiant aura, beauty's refrain,
A symphony of grace in every domain.
With each step, she paints the world anew,
In her presence, all dreams come true.
Her laughter, a melody, pure and bright,
In its echoes, darkness takes flight.
In her eyes, the universe finds its place,
Reflecting wonders, in every embrace.
With every word, she weaves stories untold,
In her essence, warmth unfolds.
In her touch, tranquility softly flows,
In her embrace, all worries repose.
Her kindness, a beacon in the night's embrace,
Guiding hearts toward a peaceful space.
In her being, love finds its home,
In her essence, we cease to roam.
So here, in this verse, I quietly impart,
Admiration for her, from the depths of my heart.
For she is the muse of life's sweet symphony,
In her presence, all is serenity.

In the Whispering Winds of Admiration

In the whispering winds of admiration's sway,
Resides a beauty that brightens the day.
With each gentle breeze, she casts her spell,
In her presence, all doubts dispel.
Her laughter, a melody, gentle and clear,
In its echo, joy draws near.
In her eyes, the stars find their gleam,
Reflecting the wonders of a dream.
With every word, she paints a scene so bright,
In her aura, all worries take flight.
In her touch, tranquility softly glows,
In her embrace, love endlessly flows.
Her kindness, a guiding light in the night,
Leading hearts toward hope's resplendent light.
In her being, love finds its truest form,
In her essence, we weather any storm.
So here, in this verse, I softly convey,
Admiration for her, in every way.
For she is the muse of life's sweet serenade,
In her presence, all fears fade.

In Her Majesty's Grace

In her majesty's grace, a marvel unfolds,
A beauty timeless, as ancient stories told.
With each graceful step, she commands the earth,
In her presence, all finds its worth.
Her laughter, a melody that dances on the breeze,
In its echo, all worries cease.
In her eyes, the stars find their guiding light,
Reflecting the wonder of the night.
With every word, she weaves a tale so grand,
In her aura, dreams take a stand.
In her touch, serenity softly flows,
In her embrace, love eternally grows.
Her kindness, a beacon in the darkest night,
Guiding souls toward hope's bright light.
In her being, love finds its home,
In her essence, we cease to roam.
So here, in this verse, I softly impart,
Admiration for her, from the depths of my heart.
For she is the muse of life's enchanting dance,
In her presence, we find our chance.

Amidst Her Radiant Glow

Amidst her radiant glow, a beauty divine,
A presence enchanting, like aged wine.
With each gentle sway, she paints the air,
In her aura, all worries repair.
Her laughter, a melody, sweet and pure,
In its echo, hearts find their cure.
In her eyes, the universe finds its gleam,
Reflecting the beauty of a cherished dream.
With every word, she spins tales untold,
In her essence, mysteries unfold.
In her touch, tranquility softly flows,
In her embrace, love endlessly grows.
Her kindness, a beacon in the darkest night,
Guiding souls toward hope's guiding light.
In her being, love finds its abode,
In her essence, hearts overflowed.
So here, in this verse, I quietly convey,
Admiration for her, in every way.
For she is the muse of my soul's sweet song,
In her presence, I feel I belong.

Enshrined in Elegance

Enshrined in elegance, she graces the stage,
A vision of beauty that none can gauge.
With each gentle step, she paints a scene,
In her presence, life feels serene.
Her laughter, a melody, soft and bright,
In its resonance, all worries take flight.
In her eyes, the universe finds its place,
Reflecting the wonders of time and space.
With every word, she weaves a tale divine,
In her aura, all troubles resign.
In her touch, serenity gently glows,
In her embrace, love endlessly flows.
Her kindness, a beacon in the darkest night,
Guiding souls toward the guiding light.
In her being, love finds its home,
In her essence, all fears are shone.
So here, in this verse, I humbly impart,
Admiration for her, straight from the heart.
For she is the muse of life's sweet refrain,
In her presence, all is pure gain.

In the Glow of Your Grace

In the glow of your grace, a symphony unfolds,
A mesmerizing beauty, the world beholds.
With each graceful stride, you paint the air,
In your presence, all troubles, I dare not dare.
Your laughter, a gentle breeze, so serene,
In its melody, a tranquil scene.
In your eyes, the stars find their gleam,
Reflecting the beauty of a cherished dream.
With every word, you cast a spell so rare,
In your essence, love fills the air.
In your touch, serenity finds its place,
In your embrace, all fears efface.
Your kindness, a beacon in the darkest night,
Guiding lost souls toward hope's light.
In your being, love finds its truest home,
In your essence, we cease to roam.
So here, in this verse, I softly impart,
Admiration for you, straight from my heart.
For you are the muse of my sweet refrain,
In your presence, I blush, and all is gain.

In Your Radiant Presence

In your radiant presence, beauty unfolds,
A sight so enchanting, my heart holds.
With each graceful move, you paint the scene,
In your aura, all troubles deem.
Your laughter, a melody, soft and sweet,
In its embrace, all worries deplete.
In your eyes, the universe finds its glow,
Reflecting the beauty only you know.
With every word, you weave a tale divine,
In your essence, love intertwines.
In your touch, tranquility gently flows,
In your embrace, all worries repose.
Your kindness, a beacon in the darkest night,
Guiding souls toward love's guiding light.
In your being, love finds its truest form,
In your essence, hearts forever warm.
So here, in this verse, I softly convey,
Admiration for you, in every way.
For you are the muse of my tender heart,
In your presence, even stars blush to impart.

Under Your Captivating Spell

Under your captivating spell, a wonder unfurls,
A sight so enchanting, it bewitches and twirls.
With every graceful movement, you command the stage,
In your presence, the world finds its adage.
Your laughter, a symphony, soft and serene,
In its delicate notes, all worries demean.
In your eyes, the stars find their gleam,
Reflecting the beauty of a cherished dream.
With every word, you cast a spell so divine,
In your essence, love and grace entwine.
In your touch, serenity softly flows,
In your embrace, tranquility grows.
Your kindness, a guiding light in the darkest night,
Leading souls toward hope's bright light.
In your being, love finds its truest form,
In your essence, hearts forever warm.
So here, in this verse, I humbly convey,
Admiration for you, in every possible way.
For you are the muse of my poetic quill,
In your presence, even silence stands still.

In the Glow of Your Grace

In the glow of your grace, a celestial dance,
A vision of beauty, a timeless romance.
With each gentle step, you paint the sky,
In your presence, all troubles bid goodbye.
Your laughter, a melody, soft and serene,
In its soothing embrace, all worries glean.
In your eyes, the stars find their gleam,
Reflecting the wonder of a dream.
With every word, you spin tales so divine,
In your essence, love and grace entwine.
In your touch, serenity softly flows,
In your embrace, tranquility glows.
Your kindness, a beacon in the darkest night,
Guiding lost souls toward hope's guiding light.
In your being, love finds its truest form,
In your essence, all hearts feel warm.
So here, in this verse, I softly convey,
Admiration for you, in every way.
For you are the muse of my tender rhyme,
In your presence, even blushes chime.

Enchanted by Your Grace

Enchanted by your grace, the world seems to sway,
A vision of beauty that brightens my day.
With each graceful move, you paint a scene divine,
In your presence, all worries seem to resign.
Your laughter, a melody, soft and sweet,
In its soothing embrace, all troubles retreat.
In your eyes, the stars find their shining light,
Reflecting the magic of a tranquil night.
With every word, you spin tales of delight,
In your essence, everything feels just right.
In your touch, serenity gently glows,
In your embrace, all fears decompose.
Your kindness, a beacon in the darkest night,
Guiding lost souls towards hope's guiding light.
In your being, love finds its truest form,
In your essence, hearts feel forever warm.
So here, in this verse, I humbly express,
Admiration for you, in every caress.
For you are the muse of my poetic rhyme,
In your presence, even time feels sublime.

In the Elegance of Your Presence

In the elegance of your presence, a marvel unfolds,
A beauty so captivating, a tale yet untold.
With each graceful step, you illuminate the way,
In your aura, all darkness seems to sway.
Your laughter, a melody, gentle and pure,
In its enchanting echo, all troubles find cure.
In your eyes, the stars find their twinkling gleam,
Reflecting the magic of a mesmerizing dream.
With every word, you paint pictures so divine,
In your essence, love and grace intertwine.
In your touch, serenity softly abounds,
In your embrace, all worries are drowned.
Your kindness, a beacon in the night's embrace,
Guiding lost souls to a tranquil space.
In your being, love finds its eternal home,
In your essence, hearts cease to roam.
So here, in this verse, I softly confess,
Admiration for you, in every caress.
For you are the muse of my heart's sweet song,
In your presence, all feelings belong.

In Your Ethereal Presence

In your ethereal presence, beauty unfurls,
A sight so captivating, it enraptures the world.
With each graceful movement, you weave a spell,
In your aura, all troubles quell.
Your laughter, a melody, soft and serene,
In its gentle cadence, all worries demean.
In your eyes, the stars find their shimmering light,
Reflecting the magic of a starry night.
With every word, you paint pictures divine,
In your essence, love and grace entwine.
In your touch, serenity softly glows,
In your embrace, tranquility flows.
Your kindness, a beacon in the darkest night,
Guiding lost souls toward hope's guiding light.
In your being, love finds its truest form,
In your essence, hearts forever warm.
So here, in this verse, I softly impart,
Admiration for you, straight from the heart.
For you are the muse of my poetic rhyme,
In your presence, even time feels sublime.

With Every Word

In the glow of your grace, the world finds its light,
A beauty so divine, it shines ever bright.
With each gentle step, you grace the earth's floor,
In your presence, all worries are shown the door.
Your laughter, a melody, soft and serene,
In its gentle embrace, all troubles are weaned.
In your eyes, the stars find their sparkling gleam,
Reflecting the beauty of a tranquil dream.
With every word, you spin tales so sweet,
In your essence, all troubles retreat.
In your touch, serenity softly flows,
In your embrace, all worries decompose.
Your kindness, a beacon in the night's embrace,
Guiding lost souls to a peaceful place.
In your being, love finds its purest form,
In your essence, hearts forever warm.
So here, in this verse, I softly declare,
Admiration for you, beyond compare.
For you are the muse of my heart's sweet refrain,
In your presence, even blushes are vain.

In the Aura of Your Charm

In the aura of your charm, the world takes flight,
A beauty so captivating, it steals the night.
With each gentle sway, you cast a spell,
In your presence, all seems well.
Your laughter, a melody, sweet and pure,
In its gentle flow, all fears find cure.
In your eyes, the stars find their gleam,
Reflecting the beauty of a dream.
With every word, you weave tales divine,
In your essence, love and grace entwine.
In your touch, serenity softly glows,
In your embrace, all worries decompose.
Your kindness, a beacon in the darkest night,
Guiding lost souls toward the light.
In your being, love finds its purest form,
In your essence, hearts feel warm.
So here, in this verse, I softly convey,
Admiration for you, in every way.
For you are the muse of my soul's sweet song,
In your presence, even blushes belong.

Unfolds

In the radiance of your presence, a wonder unfolds,
A beauty so divine, it transcends all molds.
With each graceful step, you paint the air,
In your aura, all worries are rare.
Your laughter, a melody, gentle and bright,
In its soothing rhythm, all troubles take flight.
In your eyes, the stars find their twinkling gleam,
Reflecting the magic of a blissful dream.
With every word, you spin tales of grace,
In your essence, love finds its place.
In your touch, serenity gently flows,
In your embrace, all fears quietly go.
Your kindness, a beacon in the night's embrace,
Guiding lost souls to a peaceful space.
In your being, love finds its truest form,
In your essence, hearts feel reborn.
So here, in this verse, I softly express,
Admiration for you, in tenderness.
For you are the muse of my heart's sweet song,
In your presence, all feels right and strong.

In Her Grace

In the aura of your grace, a symphony plays,
A melody so enchanting, it steals the days.
With each gentle sway, you charm the air,
In your presence, all seems fair.
Your laughter, a melody, soft and serene,
In its gentle cadence, all worries demean.
In your eyes, the stars find their gleam,
Reflecting the beauty of a dream.
With every word, you weave tales so fine,
In your essence, love and grace entwine.
In your touch, serenity softly flows,
In your embrace, all fears decompose.
Your kindness, a beacon in the darkest night,
Guiding lost souls toward hope's guiding light.
In your being, love finds its truest form,
In your essence, all storms transform.
So here, in this verse, I softly convey,
Admiration for you, in every way.
For you are the muse of my heart's sweet song,
In your presence, all is where I belong.

A tale unfurl

In her grace, a tale unfurls,
A beauty that outshines the pearls.
With each gentle smile, she paints the day,
In her presence, worries fade away.
Her laughter, a melody so sweet,
In its embrace, hearts skip a beat.
In her eyes, the stars find their glow,
Reflecting the magic only she can bestow.
With every word, she weaves a rhyme,
In her aura, all troubles resign.
In her touch, tranquility flows,
In her embrace, love eternally grows.
So here, in this verse, I softly convey,
Admiration for her, come what may.
For she is the muse of my poetic art,
In her presence, she captures every heart.

A Smile's Tale

Begins a tale with a simple smile,
A touch so sweet, it transcends the mile.
Every scent, every hue, whispers of her grace,
Leaving hearts enchanted in her embrace.
In her laughter lies an enchanting spell,
A symphony of joy, where all worries dwell.
In her eyes, a depth as vast as the sea,
Where dreams find home, where souls roam free.
Each word from her lips, a story to unfold,
A melody of love, in every word told.
In her touch, a warmth that softly beams,
In her embrace, a haven where love gleams.
Her gentle words, like a love-filled plea,
Captivate all, setting every spirit free.
In her fragrance, a sweet intoxication,
A rainbow of dreams, a vivid imagination.
This poem holds the essence of her charm,
Reading it, hearts ignite with love's warm.
A testament to her, who fills life's space,
With every verse, she leaves a lasting trace.

Love Unfolds

In whispers of love, a tale unfolds,
A narrative of hearts, where passion molds.
With each gentle word, her magic unfurls,
In her presence, love's flag unfurls.
Her laughter, a symphony, joyous and bright,
In its melody, all darkness takes flight.
In her eyes, a universe of dreams,
Where hope reigns supreme, and love beams.
With every whisper, love's song is sung,
In her essence, hearts are forever young.
In her touch, serenity takes flight,
In her embrace, everything feels right.
Her kindness, a beacon in the night's embrace,
Guiding lost souls to a peaceful space.
In her being, love finds its truest form,
In her essence, all fears are gone.
So here, in this whisper, love's story is told,
Admiration for her, in every word bold.
For she is the muse of hearts that yearn,
In her presence, love's fire will forever burn.

A Serenade of Adoration

In a serenade of adoration, love finds its voice,
A melody of affection, where hearts rejoice.
With each tender note, her essence shines,
In her presence, love's flame intertwines.
Her laughter, a sonnet of joy and delight,
In its sweet refrain, all worries take flight.
In her eyes, a kaleidoscope of dreams,
Where passion ignites, and hope gleams.
With every verse, love's tale is spun,
In her aura, a dance of hearts begun.
In her touch, tranquility finds its place,
In her embrace, all fears find solace.
Her kindness, a guiding light in the dark,
Leading souls to love's eternal spark.
In her being, love finds its purest form,
In her essence, all hearts are warm.
So here, in this serenade, love's ode is sung,
Admiration for her, forever young.
For she is the muse of love's sweet song,
In her presence, hearts forever belong.

Whispers of the Heart

In whispers of the heart, her tale is told,
A story of love, tender and bold.
With each gentle murmur, her grace unfurls,
In her presence, love's flag twirls.
Her laughter, a symphony, light and free,
In its joyful echo, all worries flee.
In her eyes, a universe of dreams resides,
Where love abides, and passion guides.
With every word, love's melody is sung,
In her essence, hearts become young.
In her touch, serenity softly flows,
In her embrace, love forever grows.
Her kindness, a beacon in the darkest night,
Guiding lost souls towards the light.
In her being, love finds its truest form,
In her essence, hearts feel warm.
So here, in whispers soft and true,
Admiration for her, in every hue.
For she is the muse of love's sweet art,
In her presence, love finds its start.

Conclusion An Epitome of Love

In the grand tapestry of life, where the threads of fate weave intricate patterns, her presence stands as a resplendent beacon, illuminating the path with the radiant glow of love's enduring essence. Through the labyrinth of time, she emerges as a timeless symbol of compassion, grace, and unwavering kindness, leaving an indelible mark on the hearts and minds of all who have been fortunate enough to cross her path.

As we draw the curtains on this narrative journey, let us take a moment to bask in the brilliance of her aura, to marvel at the depth of her spirit, and to reflect on the profound impact she has had on the tapestry of our lives. Her laughter, like the tinkling of a thousand bells, reverberates through the corridors of our memories, filling them with warmth, joy, and boundless affection.

In her eyes, we see the reflection of our deepest desires and aspirations, a mirror to the beauty and wonder that surrounds us each day. With every word she utters, she spins a tale of love and compassion, weaving together the threads of our shared humanity and drawing us closer to one another and to the essence of our own souls.

As we bid farewell to this tale of adoration and admiration, let us carry with us the timeless lessons she has imparted – to love fiercely, to laugh often, and to cherish each moment as if it were our last. For in her presence, we find not only solace and comfort but also the true meaning of love – a love that transcends the boundaries of time and space, encompassing all who are fortunate enough to experience its embrace.

And though our journey may take us far and wide, across oceans of uncertainty and mountains of challenge, her light will forever guide us home, a beacon of hope in the darkest of nights, a reminder of the beauty and wonder that exists within us all.

Thus concludes our ode to her – a tribute to the remarkable woman who has captured our hearts and inspired us to be the best version of ourselves. May her legacy endure for generations to come, a testament to the enduring power of love and the boundless capacity of the human spirit to soar to ever greater heights.

Thank You

Thank you for your kind words and for entrusting me with the task of expanding the narrative. Your appreciation and engagement fuel my creativity and drive to deliver the best possible outcome. It's truly a collaborative effort, and I'm grateful for the opportunity to work together in crafting this heartfelt expression of admiration and love.

Your input and guidance have been invaluable in shaping the narrative, and I'm honored to be part of this journey with you. If there are any other details or aspects you'd like to explore further, or if you have any additional thoughts or ideas you'd like to incorporate, please don't hesitate to share them. Your feedback is invaluable in ensuring that the final result is everything you envision and more.

Once again, thank you for your trust and collaboration. I look forward to continuing our creative partnership and bringing this narrative to its fullest expression.

In the depths of my soul, love resides,
A flame that burns with unwavering pride.
With every beat of my heart, it sings your name,
In every breath I take, your love inflames.
In the vast expanse of eternity, I find solace in your embrace,
For in your love, I discover my truest grace.
No words can capture the depth of my devotion,
For my love for you is an endless ocean.
From the depths of my being, I declare,
My love for you is beyond compare.
With every moment that passes by,
My love for you will never die.